THE
MAXWELL
JOKE BOOK

BLAKE

Published by Blake Paperbacks Ltd,
98-100 Great North Road, London N2 0NL, England

First published in Great Britain in 1992

ISBN 1 85782 007 X

British Library Cataloguing-in-Publication Data: A catalogue
record for this book is available from the British Library.

Typeset by BMD Graphics, Hemel Hempstead

Printed by Cox and Wyman, Reading, Berkshire

Cover design by Graeme Andrew

3 5 7 9 10 8 6 4 2

Foreword

At first it was no joke when the body of Mirror Group publisher Robert Maxwell was found floating in the sea off the Canary Islands on 5 November 1991 after he vanished from his luxury yacht the *Lady Ghislaine*.

Indeed, when an insensitive House of Commons journalist asked if *Daily Mirror* colleagues had heard the news about Captain Bob-bob-bob-bob he was rewarded with a smack in the mouth.

But as the weeks went by it became clear that it was Maxwell who had had the last laugh: flouting the law, bamboozling bankers, pillaging pension funds and stealing hundreds of millions.

Captain Bob had a good laugh at everyone else's expense. In this book, the laughs are on him.

Nick Yermonee,
London, 1992

A Maxwell Melody

(Sung to the tune of: "Always Look on the Bright Side of Life")

My name is Robert Maxwell, and you all think I'm dead,
You think it was my body they picked out of the Med.,
I can't say where I'm living, but I can tell you this,
Last night I met Lord Lucan and we went out on the piss . . .

> Oh, always look on the bright side of life . . .

When Kevin and Ian were small boys, they'd climb upon
  my knee,
And I would show them how to play the game "Monopoly",
Because I always cheated, I really couldn't fail,
I'd end up with all the cash and they would go to jail . . .

> Oh, always look on the bright side of life . . .

Don't blame Bob Maxwell for your plight, just blame the
  Board of Trade,
They failed to do their duty and call a spade a spade,
They said to run a company I really wasn't fit,
When what they should have said is: "Look, this man's a
  total shit . . ."

> Oh, always look on the bright side of life . . .

There's been talk of my love life, with members of my staff,
And when I read the details, I really had to laugh,
No need for you to picture me when I was on the job,
For each and every one of you's been screwed by
  Captain Bob . . .

> Oh, always look on the bright side of life . . .

Now people often wonder just how much loot I got,
I'm glad to say I saved enough to buy another yacht,
When you hear what I've called it, I know you'll all
  be stunned,
For Captain Bob is sailing on the good ship *Pension Fund* . . .

> Oh, always look on the bright side of life . . .

An old tramp came up to the Captain and complained:

"'ere, guv, I haven't had a bite in days."
So Maxwell bit him.

Maxwell introduced a whole new concept into running a company.

He called it profit-shearing.

★

Maxwell's idea of being forced to commit an unnatural act was to pay a bill

★

"Bob, you're a religious man," said Betty.

"What would you have done if you'd been at the Last Supper?"

"Asked for separate bills," growled Maxwell.

★

Maxwell was so overweight that he even made wide neckties look narrow

Maxwell was really strapped for cash just before his death.

"Look, Bob," complained his wife Betty, "we haven't paid the rent, the grocery bill, the newsagent's bill, the gas bill or the phone bill."

"Don't worry," said Maxwell. "It is always darkest before the dawn"

"It will be," said Betty. "We haven't paid the light bill either."

★

A delivery man brought a new computer to Maxwell's office and the Captain paid for it with a £500 cheque.

"Are you allowed to accept a tip?" asked Maxwell.

"Yes, I am," said the man.

"Don't try to cash the cheque," said Maxwell.

Maxwell was notoriously slow in settling bills. His office once lost the PAID stamp, and it was nine months before anyone noticed it.

★

To some of the shrewder banks in the City, Maxwell was known as Old Bedspread. Every time he asked for a loan they turned him down.

★

Maxwell called in a new lawyer and said:
    "I'll give you £50,000 if you do the worrying for me."
    "Fine," replied the lawyer. "Now, where's the £50,000?"
    "That's your first worry," said Captain Bob.

"Lend me fifty quid," asked Maxwell.

"Sorry," said his business chum. "I've only got forty."

"That's all right," said Captain Bob. "Let me have the forty and you can owe me the other ten."

"Lend me £10," Maxwell asked one of his staff.

"Sorry, sir, I can't spare that much," said the worker.

"All right," said Captain Bob. "Lend me £10, but only give me £5 now. Then I'll owe you £5 and you'll owe me £5 and we'll call it quits."

As a kid, Maxwell was very unpopular. His parents had to tie a lamb chop to his leg so the dog would play with him.

"I'd like some rat poison," said Maxwell.
  "Certainly, sir," said the shop assistant.
"Shall I wrap it up, or will you eat it here?"

Maxwell's parents didn't like him much.

When he went to school, they used to wrap his sandwiches in a road map.

★

"Whenever I'm down in the dumps I buy new clothes'" said Maxwell.

"So that's where he gets them," said one of his editors.

★

Betty was delighted when Maxwell proposed to her.

"Now we are engaged," she said, "I hope you'll give me a ring."

"Of course," said the Captain. "What's your number?"

"Do you like my company?" asked the very attractive woman executive.

"I don't know," said Maxwell. "Which company are you with?"

When the kids were small, Maxwell used to go outside on Christmas Eve, fire a shotgun in the air and then tell the children Santa Claus had commited suicide.

A down-and-out accosted the Captain and said: "I haven't had more than one meal a day all week, guv."

"I wish I had your willpower." said Maxwell.

Outside Maxwell's Oxfordshire home at Headington Hall was a sign which said: "Dogs Beware, Vicious Man!"

★

Maxwell always said that when he grew up he wanted to have a million pounds and a big house with no bathrooms. Then he could be filthy rich.

★

One of Maxwell's most successful publishing ventures was a new book called *How to be Happy without Money*. It cost £25.

★

What's six inches long and very soggy? Bob Maxwell's cigar.

What has Robert Maxwell got in common with an Essex girl?

They both go on holiday and get picked up around the Canary Islands.

As a schoolboy, Maxwell was not very good at exams. His teacher always predicted that he'd end up below C-level.

Captain Bob always said that business is like sex. When it's good, it's wonderful. When it's bad, it's still pretty good.

Maxwell moved in the best circles but never actually went straight.

Maxwell was being driven along the Embankment in London when he spotted a familiar figure slumped on a bench on the pavement. The man was bearded and scruffy, wrapped in newspapers to try and keep warm on a biting winter day. Maxwell recognised him as an old business rival.

Ordering his chauffer to stop the Rolls, Maxwell wound down the window and shouted to the tramp: "Ralph! What are you doing here, living like an old dosser?"

The man shrugged. "It's a long story, Bob. Business went bust in the recession, the debts piled up, I started drinking heavily. I lost my house, my family, my car...."

"I hate to see you like this," said Maxwell. "As you can see, I'm doing very well myself. Let me do something for you."

"Look, Bob," said the man, "if you really want to help, you can give me £10 for a bed."

"Certainly!" boomed the Captain. "Anything for an old friend. Bring the bed round in the morning and I'll have a look at it."

Maxwell weighed himself on one of those old-fashioned machines that delivers a card with your fortune printed on it.

As the ticket emerged, Betty took it and observed:

"It says you are honest, kind, generous and trustworthy."

Then she turned the ticket over and added:

"It's got your weight wrong, as well."

"Could I have Wednesday off?" asked Captain Bob's secretary. "It's my silver wedding anniversary."

"Jesus Christ!" snarled Maxwell. "Do I have to put up with this every twenty-five years?"

One of Maxwell's managers asked for a rise, but the great man turned him down and explained: "Business is bad just now, and I just can't afford it."

"But I'm doing three men's work, and always have," protested the executive.

"Three men's work!" stormed Maxwell. "Tell me who the other two men are, and I'll fire them!"

Maxwell's daughter, Ghislaine, always said that the nice thing about money is that it never clashes with anything you're wearing.

The Papworth Hospital transplant unit put in a bid for Maxwell's heart. It's not often they can get one that's hardly been used.

★

Suggestions that Maxwell committed suicide were strengthened when one of his staff recalled that a few nights before he died, Captain Bob approached by a Salvation Army worker who said: "I'm collecting for the Lord."

"Well, give me the tin," growled Maxwell. "I'll be seeing him before you."

★

What's got four wheels, weights twenty-two stone and nicks your pension fund?
Robert Maxwell on a skateboard.

Captain Bob and a few of his executives were sitting around talking one night and the conversation turned to poetry.

"The finest poets come from Scotland," boasted one director.

"Oh, really," said Maxwell. "Do you like Burns?"

"I certainly do," replied the director.

"Good," said Maxwell. Then he stubbed out his cigar on the bloke's neck.

★

Maxwell took off all his clothes one night and paraded naked in front of the bedroom window.

"Come to bed before the neighbours see you," pleaded Betty.

"They'll think I only married you for your money."

Maxwell hated people smoking, and one day encountered a young man puffing away in the corridor. He was infuriated when the youngster refused to put out the cigarette.

"How much do you earn?" roared Maxwell.

"About £150 a week." said the smoker.

Maxwell reached in his pocket and peeled off some notes. "Here's £300, for two weeks' notice," he said. "I never want to see you again. Understand?"

The young man took the money and ran down the stairs hugging himself with glee. He didn't work for Maxwell, and had only come in to deliver a parcel.

MAX FACT · TRUE STORIES

"Don't worry. You are losing sleep and that is not right. You will receive everything."

(Robert Maxwell, speaking two days before his death to Mirror Group financial director Lawrence Guest, who had questioned him about £47 million missing from company funds.)

As a youngster, Maxwell was always trying to make money, and one day he set up a little stall outside his house.

"Want to buy a toothbrush for £1?" he asked a neighbour.

"A toothbrush for £1" said the man. "Certainly not. That's daylight robbery."

"Well, then," said Maxwell. "How about a piece of home-made chocolate cake for 2p?"

"That's more like it," said the neighbour. He handed over the money, took a bite from the cake, and then spat it out in disgust.

"This cake tastes like shit!" he protested.

"It is," said Maxwell. "Wanna buy a toothbrush?"

Feelish peckish while driving to a business appointment up north, Maxwell ordered his chauffer to find the nearest fish and chip shop. When the driver failed to find one immediately, Maxwell became impatient and ordered him to pull up at a bus stop where a woman was waiting. "She'll know," said Captain Bob.

The woman said there was one in the next town and was giving directions when Maxwell said: "Get in, and you can take us there."

The startled woman climbed into the Rolls and directed them to the fish shop where Maxwell rushed in, barged his way to the front of the queue and ordered three portions for himself.

He climbed back into the car, slamming the door and leaving the woman on the pavement. She banged angrily on the window and protested: "But I live miles away from here."

Maxwell wound down the window, handed her a fiver and drove off laughing uproariously.

MAX FACT   TRUE STORY

Maxwell tore the heart out of Derby County football club and one supporter was so incensed that he forced his way into the directors' box and punched Captain Bob in the face.

People fondly remember it as the day the fan hit the shit.

Maxwell's relatives gathered for the reading of his will.

"Being of sound mind," read his lawyer, "I spent every penny before I died,"

When Kevin Maxwell was at school, the maths teacher asked him: "If your father borrowed £200 and promised to pay it back at £10 a week, how much would he owe at the end of eight weeks?"

"Two hundred pounds," said Kevin.

"You don't know your mathematics," scolded the teacher.

"You don't know my father," said Kevin.

Some of his business associates thought it quite appropriate that Maxwell should be lost at sea. They always said he was the sort of bloke who would throw a drowning man both ends of a rope.

Maxwell was approached by a young man who wanted to marry his daughter, Ghislaine. "I see no reason why you shouldn't marry her, if you can support a family," said Maxwell.

"I'm prepared to do that, sir," replied the suitor.

"Good," said Captain Bob, holding out his hand. "Counting Ghislaine, there are seven of us."

★

"You can't help liking Mr. Maxwell," said one of his secretaries. "If you don't, he fires you..."

★

"Do I smell booze on your breath?" growled Maxwell to one of his managers.

"Yes," said the executive. "I've just been celebrating the twentieth anniversary of that rise you gave me."

When he was making his way as a young businessman, Maxwell spotted oil tycoon Paul Getty in the lobby of the Savoy Hotel.

"Mr. Getty," said Maxwell. "Look, I know you don't know me, but I wonder if you could do me a favour? I am trying to complete a very big business deal with those gentlemen at the table in the corner. If you could just come over while I am talking to them and pretend to know me, then just say hello, it would impress them tremendously. My name is Bob Maxwell."

Impressed by young Maxwell's enthusiasm and initiative, Getty agreed. A few minutes later, when Maxwell was deep in conversation with the businessmen, Getty wandered over.

"Why Bob!" said the oilman. "My old friend! Good to see you again."

Maxwell looked up in annoyance. "Not now, Paul," he said "Can't you see I'm busy?"

MAX FACT   TRUE STORY

Maxwell was lunching with several top businessmen at the Savoy Hotel when he asked a waiter to bring a telephone to the table.

Asking the businessmen to keep their conversation down, Maxwell pulled a piece of paper from his pocket and dialled a number. "President Reagan?" he barked into the phone. "Robert Maxwell here. Yes, fine. How are you? Good. Listen, about that Middle East business, I have been in touch with the parties concerned and I think I am going to be able to swing it. I've called the Kremlin to put them in the picture, and I shall be going to Number 10 later tonight to bring the Prime Minister up to date. Yes, OK, I'll be in touch."

While the businessmen looked on in amazement, Maxwell put down the phone and continued his lunch.

Minutes later, Maxwell made his excuses and hurried off. But he left behind the piece of paper with the telephone number he had dialled.

Out of curiosity, one of the businessmen pocketed it and called the number when he got back to his office.

It was the talking clock.

MAX FACT   TRUE STORY

A gunman got by security, walked into Maxwell's office and demanded: "Give me all your money!"

Maxwell said: "Take the books, too. I'm £20 million short."

★

A down-and-out sidled up to Captain Bob and said: "Mister, I haven't tasted food for a week."

"Don't worry," said Maxwell. "It still tastes the same."

★

An executive limped into the *Daily Mirror* with a badly bruised foot.

"Don't worry," said Maxwell. "I'll have you walking within an hour."

Then he confiscated the man's company car.

"I think Maxwell was born with a silver spoon in his mouth," said one of his directors.

"If he was," sneered a second executive, "I bet there were somebody else's initials on it."

When Maxwell left on his ill-fated trip to the Canary Islands, one of his secretaries inquired: "Has he gone to take a rest?"

"No," said an office worker, "he's gone away to avoid it."

Two tourists were having difficulty in finding Maxwell's grave on the Mount of Olives in Jerusalem.

"Maybe," said one, "he's put it in his wife's name."

"Did you manage to set up the fire insurance policy you wanted?" Maxwell asked a shady business partner.

"No," said the businessman. "They offered to give me earthquake insurance instead, but I turned them down."

"I don't blame you," said Maxwell. "It's very hard to start a convincing earthquake."

Maxwell was having dinner with a business associate who said: "There are hundreds of ways to make a fortune, but only one honest way."

"And what's that?" demanded Maxwell.

"Aah," smiled the business, "I thought you wouldn't know!"

Maxwell walked into the *Daily Mirror* soon after he bought the business and said: "This is my son, Kevin. He's going to start at the bottom for a few days."

On the night before he died, Maxwell was in a Spanish restaurant and complained:

"This soup isn't fit for a pig."

"Sorry, sir," said the waiter. "I'll take it back, and bring you some that is."

A Mirror Group pensioner was making love to his wife when, in the throes of passion, she began screaming: "Maxwell, Maxwell!"

"Don't stop," panted the husband. "I love it when you talk dirty."

As a small boy, Kevin came bouncing into the room and asked: "Daddy, can I have another apple?"

"Another one?" growled Maxwell. "Listen, where do you think all these apples come from? You think they grow on trees?"

"Why do people take an instant dislike to me?" asked Maxwell.

"It saves time." said Betty.

Maxwell and two business associates were gathered around an open coffin, mourning the loss of a mutual friend.

The first businessman said: "There is a tradition in my family that if you place a small amount of money in the casket so it is buried with the body, it will ease the way into the next world."

And, with a flourish, he placed a £10 note on the dead man's chest.

The second businessman said: "I haven't come across this before, but it is a superstition I will happily go along with."

A second £10 note was place inside.

Maxwell spread his arms and said: "This is just the kind of generous gesture towards an old friend that appeals to me."

Then he produced his cheque book, wrote a cheque for £30, placed it alongside the dead man and took the two £10 notes as change.

Maxwell introduced a new pension plan into the Mirror Group. As with so many of his proposals, on paper it sounded very attractive, with generous benefits. But a strict condition was that it would be introduced only if every employee accepted within a week.

All the workers signed except Alf in the transport department. "It's too complicated," he said, "and I don't understand it."

Despite pressure from colleagues and union officials, Alf refused to sign.

As the deadline approached, the man was ushered into Maxwell's office. A copy of the pension plan was on the desk.

"Alf," said Maxwell, "we are on the tenth floor of this building. If you do not sign this document before I count to ten, I will throw you out of the window."

Without waiting for Maxwell to start counting, Alf signed.

"There," beamed Maxwell. "Now why couldn't you have signed this pension plan before?"

Said Alf: "Because you're the first person who explained it clearly."

Betty shivered beneath the bedclothes and said: "God, it's cold."

Maxwell, lying beside her, said: "In bed, Betty, you may call me Bob."

When Ian was young he came home in great excitement and said "Daddy, I ran home behind the bus all the way and saved 10p."

Maxwell clipped him round the ear and snapped: "Idiot! Why couldn't you have run behind a taxi and saved a pound?"

People never knew what to get Maxwell for Christmas. What do you give a man who's had everybody?

The last time Maxwell was in hospital, he got get-well cards from all the nurses.

★

Maxwell was walking along a cliff-top when he slipped and fell over the edge. An anxious aide peered down and shouted to see if his boss had survived.

"Is he still alive?" inquired a second assistant.

"Well, he said he is," said the aide. "But he's such a liar I don't know whether to believe him."

★

Every Mirror Group pensioner who goes to Israel is being asked to uproot a tree in Maxwell's honour.

Maxwell went to visit a friend in Spain who welcomed him and said: "My house is your house."

So Maxwell went out and sold it.

Maxwell hated people smoking, and constantly nagged one of his managers to quit the habit. Finally the man gave in and dumped the last of his cigarettes in the bin.

"Well done," beamed Maxwell. "Now, since you won't be needing it, I'll give you £5 for your gold lighter,"

Maxwell was on his way to his first million after he made a big killing in the City. He shot his stockbroker.

Maxwell was in his office with one of his editors when the phone rang and the editor picked it up. It was a peer of the realm, whom Maxwell had never met but had been trying to contact because he thought he could help him swing a business deal.

"What's his name?" hissed Maxwell.

"Er, Lord Ponsonby," said the editor.

"No, idiot, I mean his *full* name," snapped Maxwell. "Quick, look it up in *Who's Who*."

The flustered editor frantically riffled through the pages and then said: "Ah, here it is. Lord William St. John Fitzgibbon Ponsonby of Tadcaster and Humber."

Maxwell snatched the phone. "Hello, Bill," he boomed. "How's business?"

Maxwell was so huge that he didn't have elastic in his underpants. Just swish-rail.

★

What's the difference between Maxwell and Popeye?
   Maxwell got to Mount Olive first.

★

"They say that Jews are mean, avaricious and greedy," said Maxwell. "If I had a tenner for every time I've heard that . . ."

Maxwell wasn't a man who was easily impressed. On a visit to Texas, he asked a cattleman just how big his ranch was.

"Well," drawled the rancher, "I can get in my car, drive all day, all night and half the following day and I'll still be on my own property."

"Hmmmm," said Maxwell, "I used to have a car like that."

"I call it telephone terrorism. You say what you want to say, and then cut them off. Never forget. Phone down quickly. It always works."

(Robert Maxwell explaining his telephone technique to former Daily Mirror *editor Roy Greenslade.)*

MAX FACT   TRUE STORIES

"Notwithstanding Mr. Maxwell's acknowledged abilities and energy, he is not in our opinion a person who can be relied upon to exercise proper stewardship of a publicly quoted company."

(Department of Trade report on Maxwell's business dealings in 1970.)

MAX FACT   TRUE STORIES

"I am not a member of the Salvation Army and never have been. Basically, I'm a hard-nosed businessman."

(Robert Maxwell, 1990.)

The bloke who invented slow-motion filming got the idea after watching Maxwell pick up the bill in a restaurant.

★

Maxwell stayed in a really luxurious hotel in Paris. The bath towels were so fluffy, he could hardly shut his suitcase.

★

At Maxwell's home in Oxford the first sign of summer was when he threw his Christmas tree away.

★

Ian Maxwell once got an empty box for Christmas when he was small. Captain Bob told him it was an Action Man deserter.

Maxwell: "I'm a self-made man."

Business rival: "It's very brave of you to accept responsibility."

MAX FACT   TRUE STORY

Maxwell was showing *Daily Telegraph* editor Max Hastings around Headington Hall in Oxford when he pointed to a huge stained-glass window.

"I bet you a bottle of champagne you can't tell me what biblical scene that depicts," challenged Maxwell.

"Samson at the gates of Gaza," responded Hastings.

"Somebody must have told you!" shouted an enraged Maxell.

"No," said the editor. "Just the benefits of a sound religious education."

Maxwell grunted, and started downstairs. "I always pay my debts," he said.

A few minutes later he returned with a bottle of beer.

"And to think they let a rogue like me stay here!"

(Robert Maxwell, on discovering that previous residents of his Presidential suite in the Waldorf Towers on New York's Park Avenue included the Queen and Emperor Hirohito of Japan.)

MAX FACT   TRUE STORY

★

Financial journalist Ivan Fallon invited Maxwell to lunch, but just as Fallon and the other guests sat down, Maxwell telephoned.

"I'm sorry, but I can't make it," said Captain Bob. "I had some urgent business, and I am in Bucharest."

Fallon commiserated and told Maxwell that he was missing a splended get-together, as the guests included some of the top banking names in the City. Maxwell listened as Fallon went over the guest list and then said: "Hold on a moment."

There was a brief silence and then Maxwell came back on the line.

"I'll be round in ten minutes," he said.

How could you tell when Maxwell was lying?

His lips moved.

★

A pub which was celebrating its fiftieth anniversary decided for one day only, to revert to pre-war prices. Beer was 3p a pint and whisky was 2p a shot. The place was packed, when someone noticed Maxwell sitting alone and empty-handed in a corner.

"Not drinking, Mr. Maxwell?" inquired one customer.

"Not yet," growled Maxwell. "I'm waiting for the Happy Hour."

"If things were half as bad as some people persist in believing, I would have retired with a bottle of Scotch and a pistol a long time ago."

(Robert Maxwell responding to Department of Trade criticism in 1973.)

Maxwell never listened to his conscience. He didn't want to take advice from a total stranger.

★

Maxwell was surrounded by sharks when he fell overboard, but they refused to eat him out of professional courtesy.

★

Captain Bob was so chubby that he had mumps for six months before anyone found out.

One of Maxwell's staff was delighted to open his pay packet and find he'd been given a £20 rise.

"Thank you very much, sir," he said.

"That's all right," scowled Maxwell. "I wanted your last week here to be a happy one."

★

Maxwell was a very noisy eater. One night he was slurping soup in a restaurant and two couples got up and started dancing the cha-cha.

★

Maxwell never worried about the future. He just double-crossed every bridge when he came to it.

Maxwell staged an angry showdown with a businessman who owed him money.

"I just don't have the cash, pleaded the trader. "All I have is a watch and it only has sentimental value."

"Hand it over," said Maxwell. "I feel like a good cry."

A teenage boy was walking along a river bank when he suddenly saw someone struggling in the water. He dived in, pulled the man to safety, and was amazed to discover that the person he had saved was Robert Maxwell.

"That was a very heroic deed," boomed Captain Bob. "Do you know who I am?"

"I do indeed," nodded the teenager.

"Then you must know," said Maxwell, "that I am a very rich and influential man. If there is anything I can do to repay you, just ask."

The boy thought long and hard and said: "Well, there is one thing. I'd like to be buried in Westminster Abbey."

"Buried?" echoed Maxwell. "But you're a healthy young man."

"I know," said the youngster. "But my dad works at the *Daily Mirror* and when he finds out who I've saved he'll bloody kill me."

Maxwell stipulated in his will: "I want six directors of the National Westminster Bank as pallbearers at my funeral. They've carried me so long, they may as well finish the job."

★

A lawyer sent Maxwell an overdue account, attaching a curt note which said: "This bill is one year old."
Maxwell sent it back by return of post, marked "Happy Birthday".

★

A worker in the *Mirror* maintenance department trapped his hand in a piece of machinery but didn't realise he'd lost two fingers until he tried to say goodnight to Maxwell.

It was a nice sunny day, and Maxwell was enjoying a beef sandwich and a pint of beer outside a country pub.

Sitting nearby was a lady whose dog could smell the sandwich and kept looking up at Maxwell pleadingly and whining incessantly.

"Do you mind if I throw him a bit?" inquired Captain Bob.

"Not at all," smiled the lady.

So Maxwell picked the dog up and threw him over a wall.

★

"Why can't you act like a human being?" asked a secretary.

"Sorry," said Maxwell, "I don't like imitations."

Maxwell's staff had their own early-warning system whenever his helicopter touched down on the roof of his Mirror headquarters.

Quickly the word was passed: "The Ego Has Landed."

MAX FACT   TRUE STORY

"I've a feeling that you may perhaps be thinking that you're dealing with someone who is trying to pick, pick, pick your pocket. I am not. My record speaks for itself. You are as safe with me as you would be with the Bank of England."

(Robert Maxwell talking to Sarah Keays about a deal to serialise her book on Cecil Parkinson, October 1985.)

Solly the tailor had always wanted to take up scuba-diving, so when he retired from his shop in London's East End he went out to Tenerife and took a very expensive course of lessons. He bought the very best equipment, and when he finally qualified he decided to make his first major dive off the Canary Islands. He was kitted out with all the sophisticated gear, plus a special pad and pen that could write underwater so he could jot down his impressions of life beneath the waves.

He was 100ft down in the Mediterranean when, to his amazement, he suddenly saw Robert Maxwell come floating by, wearing only a towel.

Solly swam after Maxwell, tapped him on the shoulder and scribbled on the writing pad: "How come I've spent thousands of pounds on scuba gear and you just paddle around at this depth without even a face mask?"

Captain Bob grabbed the pad and wrote: "Because I'm drowning, you prat."

Maxwell was asked for a donation to the orphanage, so he sent them two orphans.

★

Judge: "As the jury have found you not guilty of fraud, you are free to go."
Maxwell: "Does that mean I can keep the money?"

★

Maxwell just didn't know the difference between right and wrong. He thought illegal was a sick bird.

Maxwell was sitting on a crowded London underground train where three elderly ladies were standing.

Captain Bob turned to a teenager sitting next to him and said: "Young man, if you were a gentleman you'd get up and let one of those ladies sit down."

"Yes," said the youngster. "And if *you* were a gentleman you'd get up and let all three of them sit down."

★

Maxwell felt unwell after a trip abroad and went to the doctor, who told him: "I am sorry to tell you that you may have rabies, and it could prove fatal."

"In that case, you'd better give me a pencil and paper," demanded Maxwell.

"To make your will?" asked the doctor.

"No," said Captain Bob. "To make a list of the people I want to bite."

A visitor was leaving a hospital when she noticed two doctors searching in the grounds.

"Excuse me," said the woman, "have you lost something?"

"No," said one doctor. "We're doing a heart transplant for Robert Maxwell and we're looking for a suitable stone."

★

Tramp: "You haven't got 50p for a cup of coffee, have you?"

Maxwell: "You must have been speaking to my bankers."

★

Maxwell proved that the age of chiselry is not dead.

When Maxwell took over the Mirror Group he had a brilliant marketing idea. He flew to Rome to try to persuade the Pope to make a commercial.

"Look, your Holiness," said Captain Bob. "I'll pay you £500,000 for a ten-second commercial. All you have to do is face the camera and say: 'Give us this day our *Daily Mirror*.'"

"Sorry," said the Pope, "I can't do that."

"I'll make it £1 million," said Maxwell.

"The answer is still no," replied the Pope.

"Two million," urged the Captain.

"Sorry," replied the Pope.

Angry and disappointed, Maxwell left. On the flight home to London he turned to his secretary and said: "I wonder how much the bread people are paying him?"

Maxwell loved London. One of his regular habits was to stroll through Trafalgar Square, stealing food from the pigeons.

"I'd like to see something cheap in a blue suit," said Maxwell.

"Here," said the tailor. "Put this on and go and look in the mirror."

★

Maxwell walked with a bit of a limp. He broke his ankle squeezing the last of the toothpaste out of the tube.

★

Maxwell insisted that his staff stay at the very cheapest hotels when they were out of town. One hotel had a colour brochure in which the beds weren't made.

Betty Maxwell was in a spot of bother and a policeman stopped to help when he saw her standing by the roadside. "Thank you, officer," said Mrs. Maxwell. "The car had a puncture. I've managed to change the wheel, but now I can't get it down off the jack."

"No trouble, madam," said the copper. "I'll soon sort it out."

"Please lower the car gently," said Betty. "My husband is asleep on the back seat."

★

A bloke came up to Maxwell and said: "Can I tap you for a fiver?"

Said Maxwell: "For a fiver, you can hit me with a brick."

Maxwell went into the local grocer's shop and asked: "How much are your eggs?"

"They're £1.50 a dozen, but 75p if they're cracked," said the shopkeeper.

"Crack me a dozen," said Maxwell.

"You worked with Robert Maxwell. Can you describe him?"

"Yes, he was 6ft 2ins tall and £700 million short."

Maxwell called his entire office staff together to tell them a new joke he had just heard. Everyone but one man laughed uproariously.

"What's the matter with you?" snarled Maxwell. "Didn't you think that was funny?"

"I don't have to laugh," said the worker. "I'm leaving on Friday anyhow."

Maxwell was driving his Rolls-Royce when he ran out of petrol outside a village pub. Spotting an old boy drinking a pint at a table outside, Maxwell called him over and asked him to give the car a push to the local garage, which was about 500 yards away.

Puffing and panting, the old man pushed the heavy car up the steeply sloping village street to the petrol pumps, and almost collapsed when he got there.

Maxwell paid for petrol with a £10 note, then patted his pockets for a tip to give his breathless helper.

Finding he had no more money, Maxwell wound the window down and said to the pensioner: "I'm sorry, but I've spent all my cash on petrol. Do you smoke, by any chance?"

"Yes, sir I do," said the pusher.

"Well, I would give it up if I were you," said Maxwell. "You look absolutely knackered."

Then he wound up his window and drove off.

During the war, Maxwell fought with Field Marshal Montgomery. Then he fought with General Eisenhower and he also fought with General Patton. In fact, he couldn't get on with anybody.

★

A secretary arrived for work an hour late. Her clothes were torn, her face was bloodied and bruised and she had one arm in a sling.

"It's ten o'clock," screamed Maxwell. "You were supposed to be here at nine. What happened?"

"I'm sorry," explained the secretary. "I fell out of a ninth-storey window."

"This took you a whole hour?" said Maxwell.

Maxwell had a military figure – most of it was up at the front.

★

Maxwell bought his mistress an eighteen-carat gold diaphragm studded with diamonds. He liked to come into money.

★

Betty Maxwell was watching the evening news on TV and shouted to Bob: "Did you hear that: A man in London swapped his wife for a season ticket to all the Arsenal football games. Would you do a thing like that?"

"Hell, no," growled Maxwell. "The season's half over."

Who was Maxwell's favourite historical figure?

   Jack the Ripoff.

★

Maxwell was so fat that he once went to the cinema wearing a white shirt and they showed the film on his back.

★

As a schoolboy in Czechosolovakia during the war, Maxwell was running frantically through the streets of Prague, trying to avoid capture by the Germans.

   Darting down a side street, he hammered on the door of a closed grocery store. "I know it's late," he told the startled shopkeeper. "But do you think you could cache a small Czech?"

"How do I stand?" asked Maxwell.

"I don't know," said the doctor. "To me, it's a miracle."

Maxwell and a business acquaintance were walking down a dark London street when they suddenly found themselves surrounded by a gang of muggers.

"Here, take this," said Maxwell, thrusting a bundle of notes into his companion's hand. "It's the £500 I owe you."

If Maxwell and Jeremy Beadle were standing on the top of a twenty-storey building and they both jumped off at exactly the same time, which one of them would hit the ground first?

Who cares?

Maxwell was so fat that he went to Weight Watchers on a scholarship.

Maxwell hired a new manager and promised him: "I'll pay you between £440 and £450 a week." When the executive opened his first pay packet, it contained just £10.

★

Secretary: "How do I stand for a £10 rise?"
Maxwell: "You don't – you grovel."

★

Maxwell walked into a clothes shop and said: "I'd like to see a suit that would fit me."

"So would I," said the assistant.

Maxwell took a businessman to a very expensive restaurant and they were only just starting on the first course when Maxwell angrily called for the manager.

"There's a fly in my soup," complained Captain Bob loudly. "It's disgraceful. I never expected to encounter such a thing in a restaurant with a reputation like yours."

"Shhhh," pleaded the manager, looking anxiously around the crowded dining room. "These things can happen, sir. Won't you gentlemen have dinner on the house?"

After dinner the two men left and Maxwell pointed to a shop across the street. "Could you manage an ice cream?" he asked. "I've got one more fly left."

★

Barber: "Just a haircut, Mr. Maxwell, or would you like an oil change, too?"

Maxwell loved Al Jolson songs. His favourite was: "When old Captain Bobbin' comes rob-rob-robbin' along..."

★

Spanish authorities trying to piece together Maxwell's last hours are investigating a frog diver's report that there's money missing from Davy Jones's locker.

★

What's red and shiny and goes around carrying a bag of shit? Maxwell's Rolls-Royce.

Maxwell took his Rottweiler down to the local pub and got into conversation with two other dog owners.

"You know," said one of the men, "it's quite true what they say about dogs adopting the personality of their owners. And I can prove it."

Buying a packet of biscuits at the bar, the man laid them out on the floor in front of his dog. "I'm an architect," he said. "Just see what my dog does with these."

Delicately taking the biscuits one by one in his mouth, the dog stacked the biscuits on top of each other, producing a neat little tower.

"You see," beamed the architect. "He's designed a sort of building."

The second man then took the biscuits and laid them out in front of his dog. "I'm an artist," he said. "Let's see what he'll do."

Nudging the biscuits with his nose, the dog arranged them into a very artistic formation, something akin to a modern art painting.

Delighted with their pets' performances, the two men then turned to Maxwell and said: "Now it's your turn."

So Captain Bob let his Rottweiler off the leash. It bit the barman, ate the biscuits, fucked the other two dogs and ran out of the door.

★

Maxwell always paid by credit card when he went on vacation so that if the plane crashed on the way back he'd have a free holiday.

Maxwell was very lucky at cards but could never make money at the racetrack. It's hard to hide a horse up your sleeve.

★

Maxwell's career was amazing. He started off as a barefoot peasant boy and became one of the most highly suspected figures in the City.

★

Give Maxwell a free hand and he'd stick it in your pocket.

Maxwell had his first sexual experience in the back of a taxi cab in Hyde Park. He was alone at the time.

★

Maxwell bequeathed his body to science. Science is contesting the will.

★

"You're overweight," said the doctor.

"I want a second opinion," said Maxwell.

"All right," said the doctor. "You're ugly as well."

Maxwell was trying to board a bus when the Pakistani conductor barred his way.

"No more room," he said. "I'm crammed jam full."

"I don't care what your name is," barked Maxwell. "I'm coming on."

★

First secretary: "Would you kiss Mr. Maxwell under the mistletoe?"

Second secretary: "I wouldn't kiss him under anaesthetic."

When he fell into the sea off his yacht, the
sharks panicked and swam around
shouting:

"Maxwell, Maxwell!"